I0814935

Community Workers

Librarians

by Amy McDonald

BELLWETHER MEDIA
MINNEAPOLIS, MN

Blastoff! Beginners are developed by literacy experts and educators to meet the needs of early readers. These engaging informational texts support young children as they begin reading about their world. Through simple language and high frequency words paired with crisp, colorful photos, Blastoff! Beginners launch young readers into the universe of independent reading.

Sight Words in This Book

a	good	people	want
can	help	some	what
do	in	the	with
find	make	they	
for	new	use	

This edition first published in 2025 by Bellwether Media, Inc.

Library of Congress Cataloging-in-Publication Data

LC record for Librarians available at: https://lccn.loc.gov/2024037973

Editor: Betsy Rathburn Designer: Laura Sowers

Printed in the United States of America, North Mankato, MN.

Table of Contents

On the Job

The girl wants a good book. A librarian can help!

STAFF
Public Library
Create With Confidence

What Are They?

Librarians work in libraries. Some work in schools.

They help people use the library.

What Do They Do?

Librarians sort books. They make **displays**.

display

They fix
ripped books.
They order
new books.

They give **library cards**. They help people **borrow** books.

library cards

Great River Regional Library

PUBLIC LIBRARY

They make spaces for children.
They read stories.

They help with computers. They help people do **tasks**.

Why Do We Need Them?

Librarians help people find what they need!

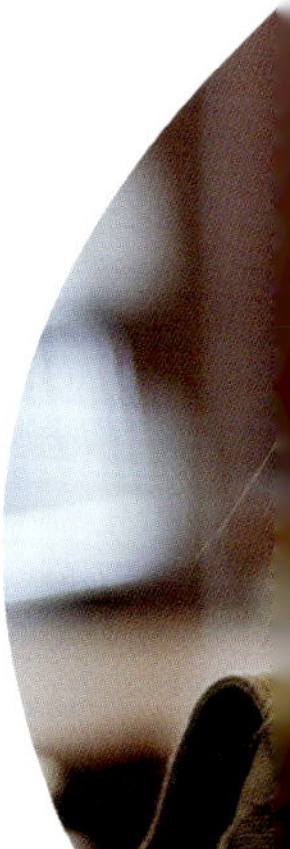

Librarian Facts

Tools

library card

computer

books

A Day in the Life

sort books

read stories

help with computers

Glossary

borrow

to take for a short time

displays

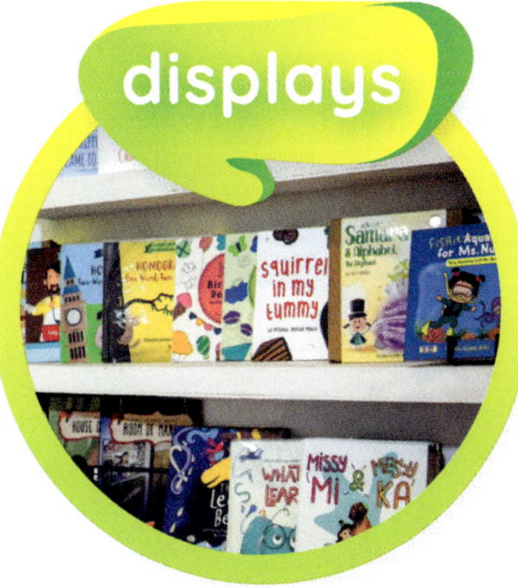

things that are set up to show others

library cards

cards that let people borrow library books

tasks

activities or jobs

To Learn More

ON THE WEB

FACTSURFER

Factsurfer.com gives you a safe, fun way to find more information.

1. Go to www.factsurfer.com.
2. Enter "librarians" into the search box and click 🔍.
3. Select your book cover to see a list of related content.

Index

The images in this book are reproduced through the courtesy of: SDI Productions, front cover, pp. 20-21, 23 (borrow, tasks); Ingrid Balabanova, p. 3; Dylanhatfield, p. 4; JGalione, pp. 4-5; knelson20, p. 6; AzmanL, pp. 6-7; Robert Kneschke, pp. 8-9; 1000Photography, p. 10; Tyler Olson, pp. 10-11; Ines Fraile, pp. 12-13; Independent Picture Service/ Alamy, p. 14; Wavebreakmedia Ltd, pp. 14-15; rido, pp. 16-17; Jim West/ Alamy, pp. 18-19; Rachael Barnes, p. 22 (library card); studiovin, p. 22 (books); GreenThumbShots, p. 22 (computer); Jacob Wackerhausen, p. 22 (sort books); wavebreakmedia, p. 22 (read stories); Brian T. Young, p. 22 (help with computers); Rahul Sapra, p. 23 (displays); T. Carter Ross/ Wikipedia, p. 23 (library cards).